city without a head

LIMITED EDITION
15 / 200

me4writers

...are a loose collective of Medway-based writers, founded in 2009 by playwright Sam Hall. They work together on text-based projects, with other artists, writers, and members of the local community.

Their events and projects have been performed, commissioned, and produced around Kent and further afield.

They were 'highly commended' in the Medway Culture and Design Awards 2012.

Writers featured in this collection of poetry and prose are; Barry Fentiman, Sam Hall, SM Jenkin, Anne-Marie Jordan, Sarah March, Tara Moyle and Roy Smith.

...me4writers.wordpress.com

city with-out a head

POETRY AND PROSE BY ME4WRITERS
EDITED BY SAM HALL

First published in 2013 by
Wordsmithery
5 Curzon Road
Chatham
Kent, ME4 5ST
www.wordsmithery.info

A CIP record for this book is available from the British Library.

Cover image and illustrations by Victoria Wainwright.

isbn 978-0-9926853-0-0
printed in the UK by Inky Little Fingers

contents

foreword

This collection of writings, thoughts and ideas grew from a project ME4Writers were invited to be part of, in 2010. Inspired by the idea of creating an oblique encyclopaedia loosely in the style of Georges Bataille's *Encyclopaedia Acephalica*, we decided to make a collaborative, alternative index putting cities under the microscope.

Cities were chosen because at the time Medway's potential (but thus far, not achieved) new city status was a hot topic.

We drew up a list of words to define, and rules to help make the collection cohesive, (see appendix). We then dismissed these rules or wrote adhering to them depending on how we felt. This first stage was part of the arts based indie pop club night *Moogie Wonderland,* on 6 November, 2010.

We decided what we had started was a good idea and that we would develop it, this time with looser observance to the rules and inviting contributions from guest writers. The resulting words were issued in eight limited edition fanzines between 2010 and 2012, *The Encyclopædia Citæcephale.*

The project continued to grow; we also perform extracts at live events and there are two possible forthcoming books, inspired by the ideas planted.

The book you have in your hands is a collection of the best writing by ME4 regulars, more than a collection of poems, prose, short stories, fragments, news stories and found writing; a collection of memories and thoughts, evoking some of the things we feel (or felt) about life in the city. A collection which grew organically, like the cities it aims to look sideways at.

Sam Hall, Editor

why does your city have no head?

Cities as we now understand them are golems. An agglomerated clay of humanity and the things that humanity drags behind it. The good, the bad and the necessary.

They have a tablet of basic instructions that were inserted somewhere so far back that the thing can no longer hear it. And neither can its people or its nominal rulers. It has limbs and arteries but its intelligence is scattered. It has no *head*.

One thousand years ago the inhabitants of these places may have clustered by a river or well for sustenance. Or in the shadow of a castle or cathedral. Indeed the qualification for citihood in the UK pre-1907 was the establishment of an Anglican cathedral.

It is why Ripon is a city and Reading which has ten times its population is not. The title 'city' has now passed from a clerical to a royal honour. A tablet with an inscription and a crest. It says 'you are a city, now go and become citizens' but it means nothing, save for a change of regalia.

Ancient piles of stone and royal proclamations matter only to chain wearers and heritage officers. Moderns cities are the creation of money, of concentrated, overt wealth.

Regardless of the badge on the sign if you are in a city then you know it. As the old saying goes: *if you have to tell someone you're important then you ain't*.

It was money that dragged the people in from the fields 200 years ago. But even money can get old.

The runes upon the tablet wear away.

Middlesbrough was little more than a farm at the

time of the first census, yet within a century was home to 90,000 people pouring into the steel mills. A perfect storm of natural resources, scientific advances, and a great river to send girders round the world to make money for men with exhuberant whiskers.

It has been a post-industrial grey blotch on the map since the 1980s. The tablet has worn smooth. There are no jobs, there is no industry. And yet the people are still there and proud of the place that they live in for all its faults.

The light may die behind the clay mask but it staggers on. A lightwell of choice and hubbub. A centripetal force on the surrounding districts, 'strings of pearls beckon us to follow them'.

Of course, one place where money never gets old is London. We bitch about it, we can't take the pace, we yearn for pastoral fictions while having coffee spilled on us on the tube, but we don't leave. It is the greatest golem of them all, it has a tablet of pure gold inscribed with a dollar sign. It is a movie set where they never shout 'cut'.

In what follows we shall take a look through the eyes of these headless conflicted creatures, these pavement actors. There are no answers for them or for us, but this is a movie that you don't want to miss.

Barry Fentiman

alienation (1)

In the early nineties, laid sideways with the volume
low, late night commercial television buzzed
in and out of reception, displaying episodic
detective fiction with generally altruistic visitors,
whose pink scalped women inspired youthful
fantasy. Solo adventures, locked in loft and
smoking from windows, gave way to half-read
subtitles and tuning expertise. Formative in
expanding a world of bungalows and structured
greenery, often motivated by prurient self-interest.

Also see: A rumour of the capital's gaming
experience, never visited, but often heard about. It
attracted boys beneath the circus with the promise
of laser guns and latex gore. I envied them.

"Excuse me, do you work here?"

The utterance that strikes terror into the heart of all temporary staff in customer service situations. This is mainly owing to the fact that there are, from my point of view, a number of answers to that question, none of which are strictly true.

For the purposes of descriptive and geographical accuracy, I am indeed working and I am also here. That said, should I answer yes to his question the chain of events that follows will almost certainly result in catastrophic damage to the ontological security of said customer.

The reason for this is that he will then reasonably expect me to be able to tell him about the products I am stacking and where others may be found. We would then be on the road to insanity as I would then be forced to admit that firstly, while I may be working, I have no idea what I am doing. My second culpable admission will be, that while I am undoubtedly here, I have no real sense of where here actually is.

The problem with this is, that to say no would be palpably absurd. I am without doubt here so far as the customer is concerned as he can see me. Also, the Satanic pact that all temporary staff make with their patrons does not allow for any admission of professional confusion. Confusion is the job of the customer and we are here to unburden them of it.

It is indeed a little known fact that the scanners on store entrances serve a double purpose. Quite apart from the detection of light-fingered clientele, it is rumoured by many in the service sector that they somehow lobotomise the individual in question back to the infantile state that is known as being a customer. Hence the face of competency must be maintained at all times lest they become more nervous than is good for them.

If the above passage is beginning to make the reader's head hurt, try actually living it on a daily basis.

In light of the above it is therefore unsurprising that my only real answer to his innocent request regarding the ordering of flowers was met by a somewhat pained expression on my part followed by a long, drawn out rendition of that well known classic:

"Errr..."

The plan goes like this...
are you listening?
Are you listening?

Sssh. Of course I am.

This is important.

...I know it is. (To you.)

We cannot be
discovered...
This is going to change
everything.
My grand design for the
future...
Realised now.

boredom

I pick the fluff out of my belly button and twirl
and whirl it, between finger and thumb, into a
ball too small for school kids to kick between
two pullovers dumped on grass as goalposts. I
graduate to flicking the grime under my fingernail
at the light fitting above my head as I loll on the
bed, waiting.

The tick tock of the alarm clock stretches
like chewing gum stuck on the sole of sweatshop
trainers and burrows into my brain like a rush hour
train crammed with caffeine-fuelled commuters.

This conveyor belt has no end

bourgeois

The defining characteristic of the nineteenth century high street builders was their overweening arrogance. To see this all one has to do is look up.

An iconography of the upper floors of any main drag outside the clone belt would show a ribbon of reliefs proclaiming in their ornate grandeur the permanence of their brand.

Drop one's eyes to ground level and it quickly becomes clear that such permanence was illusory. The old order of burghers spawned its own destruction.

The Old White Hart now grazes above a branch of *Sainsbastards*. The imperial eagle of Midland Bank (as was) proclaimed a 1,000-year Reich and is now a branch of High and Mighty.

Herr Habermas would recognise how their modernistic project was not completed through an ironic combination of hubris and lack of nerve. Beautiful stone relics passed through the wall of oblivion like their creators. As their neon usurpers surely will, yet cannot see it.

bowery

The desire to emulate Bukowski's dream masks
an immature desire to evade questions of equality
and suffering. Nevertheless, stimulating prose,
pulsing, underbelly rhythms and offhand cruelty
pass the time adequately. Repetitive, broken scenes
of grotesque, booze-fuelled love, does poverty
resist a capitalist urge? More likely the porn of
middle class voyeurs, wading through the shit of
lost souls.

Isn't it funny the way you never see white powdery dog shit on the street anymore?

Is this because the dog food manufacturers are now aware of health and safety issues of feeding our canine companions ash and other unsavoury abattoir by-products, or is it that our little woofers have now become such discerning consumers that they would turn their doggy noses up at anything less than caviar and Krug?

I will do nothing:
Refuse to operate by
antiquated rules.

capital

No-one has ever read volumes II and III.

Up until the eighteenth century a public execution was considered a good day out. In London, at Traitor's Gate it was commonplace to see the beheaded heads of anyone who had the misfortune to get on the wrong side of the monarchy. In fact it was commonplace to keep mementoes from the body of a beloved, somewhat like the relics, or saints' bones, of olden days.

Henry VIII seemed to take a particular amount of pleasure in lopping people's heads off and displaying them for all to see.

John Fisher, the Bishop of Rochester, was beheaded in 1535, for refusing to accept Henry as the head of the Church of England. Fisher's head was then boiled and stuck on a pole on London Bridge. But for the next week or more, the Bishop's head seemed to grow fresher and look healthier than when he was alive. Fearing the 'miracle' would cause dissent, Henry ordered the head to be taken down and flung into the Thames.

Sir Thomas More, a Renaissance humanist and statesman who coined the word 'utopia', also refused to sign Henry's Acts of Supremacy and Succession, so was executed and his head impaled on a pole on London Bridge, replacing that of Fisher. But after a month his head is said to have fallen from the pole into the arms of his devout daughter. She then kept the head with her in a lead box for the rest of her life.

Watching me. All the time. My image captured on average 300 times a day. Does it make me feel safe though? Can the faceless bodies watching up in their ivory towers really do anything should something happen? I have a right to my image and I can write to the company and get copies of what they hold on me. How many hundreds of times a day am I expected to do this? I am on public transport. I pick my nose or scratch my arse. Will it appear on *People do the most uncouth things!!!* (Channel 5) in two years' time?

No more having sex on the train then.

city without a head

I am the place where you live and the place that you cannot escape. I am the name of your football team and the name of the cab company that you use. I am the place that rules you and records your every movement. I am bricks and concrete and asphalt and paving slabs. I am the lonely football across the road from the Co-op waiting for someone to kick me into the derelict garage full of buddleia.

I am the place deep in your heart. I am the whispering memory deeper in the part of you called fear. I am why you cluster around the fire on cold Thursday nights when chicken wrappers blow down the street and tin cans rattle after them in pursuit. Remember the fire, the sticks, the hides, the wolves circling outside. Remember the cave. That is where I was born in you.

The priests made me stone, made me tall. I was mighty. They carved me with fierce beasts and green men inspiring awe and silence in the face of promised damnation. My stone is quiet now. It broods, it contemplates its fate. Growing black and crusted with time. Posing for photographs in new rituals where people talk and talk and talk and walk away. A rock is placed across the entrance and no-one is coming out. Gods came, gods went. Situation vacant.

Men with whiskers and attributes for names made me of brick. Wearing plaid suits they wrought the world in their image. Piling brick upon brick till the earth could only retreat. And their creatures poured forth each day at the whistle's call. But there were never enough. I grew till all was slate beyond the imagination of men.

And the great men named me for other great men
claiming a dominion that was never dark.

But the sun did set and I was named for
battles not men. And the tide of hubris that carved
emblems atop doors washed back. And the world
came to me as though in a dream. And I welcomed
them. But it got cold. My coat of pebble-dashed
ugliness could not defend me. The palindrome
came and adorned me with designer jewellery
but kept me hungry. And the people wrote their
thoughts upon me. "*Solly is a cunt*", apparently.

And in the night I shiver as the people slip away.
The woman on the television showed them how.
The others huddle by the Co-op near the ball. The
corner pub is shuttered with a tree stuck out the
gutter, there's a sticker in the window 'cross the
road: "*If this flag offends you, then maybe you should
move.*"

I think that I shall come apart if the people come
unglued.

I am the place you are stuck. The wind
whistles through windows that don't shut. I am
modernised. I have an action plan. Logos circle
in anticipation of official signage. I am demolished.
I am having a *Renaissance*. I am a *Gateway*. I am
only 40 minutes from London. They leave me
every day. I am brown steel windows. So many
dogs. I have ceased to have a purpose. They have
forgotten the cave.

I am bags fluttering in trees. *One nation under
Tesco.* I am external furniture for the kids to
play on. I am deserted after six o'clock. I am
pedestrianized to minimise casualties. I am *World
Heritage.* I am a museum. I am not in their heart

any more. They live in me but I do not live in them. There are no wolves, they only fear each other. I am having a nervous breakdown. So many dogs. Please kick the ball. I placed it for a reason. It holds my memories. It holds my past, present and future.

My time is up. The goal is open. Strike for the wilderness and let me go so that we may start again.

civic

It was yellow, with a black go-faster stripe down the sides. Automatic drive. The first car after passing my test. My mum's. I only had one little prang in it and fortunately nobody noticed.

claustrophobic

Kept safe from lashing rain in nylon chrysalis.
Surprising warmth, I hear her breathe beside me
unaware; she slept whilst I wandered. There was
little warning; a clap of thunder and then it fell, by
then we sat by a dying fire as light rose through
nighttime's end. Outside a savage freedom,
mudslide in miniature and many fortresses
destroyed, but in here we shelter with a mild
stench, some insects and our sweat.

clone-town

The centre of this STNL (small town near
London©) was swept away a good few years ago.
There's a plaque to this effect commemorating her
Majesty's blessing of the project. Let's be honest, a
lot of STNLs frankly deserve a wrecking ball to the
guts. They spewed forth from the forties' overspill
already poxed with the leisure centre virus,
stillborn, now sadly lacking any existential drive.
A thing cannot be if it no longer possesses a
purpose. This one, this one, however used to be a
proper town by all accounts. Before the soon-to-be
extended shopping complex sprung up in its place.
The headlong rush to be Basingstoke astounds me.
Is this really what people want? I watched a rugby
match on the TV in a pub in Basingstoke with a
friend of mine. They called time at 8.30pm as the
centre was closing. The word 'centre' in this case
has deliberate ambiguity.

I shop.
Therefore I am.

People who work in
The town often prefer to live
In the countryside.

concrete

the typographical
arrangement of
w o r d s
          is as impor-
tant in conveying
the intended
          effect
as the conventional
elements of the poem
such as
meaning,

          rhythm

                    and

                    RHYME

concrete jungle

We are many and our time has arrived. Cull us? You cannot even catch us.

Descended as we are from the three great families of Huston, Hendrix and Manuel, we share the blood of kings and poets. We are noble. We bring colour where there is only greyness.

Arrogant apes! You are behaving like insects.

consumerism

I want you. My life will be complete with you. My breathing speeds up when I think of you. I can't concentrate on anything except you. It's possible I will die if I can't have you. Life is a four-letter word without you. You get me up in the morning. You give my life CPR and GPS. You put the carrot into my cake. You are everywhere. You block out the sun yet provide its warmth.

You are like the rest. You suck me into your vortex with promises of passion and plenty. You vomit me out the other side with a smirk on your face. You have nothing to give but are willing to take. You offer emptiness, as if a carefully chosen present. You expect me to be grateful. You are still hungry.

I have no energy left to despise you. I should have kept that receipt. I am spent.

conurbation

Shot after shot, drink after drink, a progressive inebriation. A thousand nights weave a pattern of excess and excretion, full of heroes, derring-do and wonder. From deep within the grip, twist hard, don't ever lose the fight, but keep it real and never stop and dance until I die.

Yet looking back, those 'lost it' times are all one moment, gone forever.

They keep the Bic razor blades
Behind the counter
In my local corner shop

demo

In Hell he sat by Satan's side, whispering advice.
This fiercest fiend, who must be heard, craved
change to organisation. All had their say in
tortures' field, he consulted the conscripted. Put
to the vote, those hapless fools, the servants of the
devil, to see which had the proper skills to manage
the inferno. Some favoured blades, others the lash,
but all agreed on brimstone and they came together
in one voice to punish the transgressor. They could
never get it right by all, but hoped their best would
do. And argued long of wrong and right and
whose blood tasted true.

   The years went by and resentment grew, in
those who felt neglected, troubles stored and fires
cold when some views aren't respected. So levels
ground to unholy halt, for the workers' revolution.
Whips and sticks thrown to the ground to show
their indignation. Wrote up demands for equal
pain and holiday extension. Then from his throne
he bellowed 'what?' and they realised they weren't
sovereign.

derelict

Where is it? I know it's been a long time but I grew up down here. So much has altered. All the names have changed. Of course I knew that Woolworths was a goner. Many's the time I used to nick the pick'n'mix from there.

Such a long time ago now, but it's a slightly more recent memory I need to revisit now. Mistry's Chemist is still there, I know it was near there, the scene of much embarrassment at the time.

"Really, Steve— it doesn't matter, maybe we could just go and get a drink or something and catch up?"

"Oh, no, no, no, it was your idea to find this place. It's bound to be here somewhere."

"Hey, mate, can you tell me where Frobisher's hairdressers has got to? It should be here but somehow we keep missing it."

A slightly dishevelled chap in a cagoule and a Benny hat makes a puzzled, slightly constipated face before replying,

"Ooh, you've got me there, guv... Rings a bell it does. 'Ang on, I'll ask these two lovely ladies 'ere, two of me best customers they are, been around 'ere forever."

He gestures towards two pepper pot women queuing to get in the Post Office clutching magazines under their arms.

"Less of your cheek, young Andy!" (Young Andy is 50 if he's a day.) "Where are you looking for, lovey?"

I mention the old hairdressers and one of them lights up like a candle and turns to her partner in crime to confer. Straight away she points at an old boarded up shell of a place across the street.

There are trees growing from the guttering and brown steel over the windows. The old barber's pole has gone. Nothing left that speaks of past glories. An old Rasta sitting in the doorwell hunkered up against the elements, making a decent fist of the theme from *Midnight Cowboy* on his harmonica. Beside him, a chipped china bowl with a few quid in it guarded by a runty Jack Russell terrier. Something stirs in my memory...

"Look at the fakkin state of 'im!" interjects 'young' Andy.

"Language, Andrew!" shrieks one of the pots.

"Well I ask yer," comes the retort. "E's out 'ere every bleedin' day sat on 'is arse playin' the same tune expectin' decent people to feed 'im an 'is bloody dog, 'e should get a job!"

And with that Andy finishes his sandwich and reaches down into a bag by his feet and pulls out a bundle of magazines.

"Well folks, can't 'ang about like 'im, back to work... *BIG ISSUE*! ... *BIG ISSUE*!"

But, we're no longer listening...

"Come on, Jules, this is it, don't you remember?"

"Well, now you come to mention it, but it's all fastened up, even the alley down the side's all covered in chicken wire and stuff."

Then it hits me. I look the old busker in the eye for the first time. A black skull stares back at me, snow white dreads pulled into a filthy old tam. He's well dressed in a shabby sort of way. Harris Tweed and a now crummy silk tie.

"Mr Bishop! ... I didn't recognise you, or the shop for that matter."

"Well I remember you, boy. An' her, too. How

could I forget? Come t' think of it, how could you?"

My eyes widen and Jules blushes nearly scarlet.

"Come t' finish what I din't let ya, eh boy? Well I guess it can't hurt none now, can it?"

He grins wide and leers with his eyes to the trussed up alley entrance and subtly nudges it with his foot. It opens just enough.

And now we're trotting hand in hand past rotting bins and clammy busted drainpipes. It's all flooding back now. Twenty-four years nearly to the day. I can still feel Julie's hand on my cheek and Fro's boot up my arse. Her shame when he told her dad. Guess he's atoned for that now. And the long years in-between. Wonderful thing the internet.

And here we are again and all those years fall away. Still so beautiful. Trembling we touch fingertips.

"I... I don't know what to say now."

"You could try the same line as last time, you old smoothie."

"OK, get 'em off then!"

desolation

It'll be the early evening about Tuesdayish when it hits you. Probably just after the clocks go back. Shuffling along some chicken shop drag in the drizzle. This must be what invisibility feels like. Uncomprehending faces stare glassily at a place three feet behind your head.

The only light seems to come from gaily illuminated plastic spattered with rain and road shit. And you just implode. Not with massive import like a star collapsing, or lethally like a cathode ray tube giving up its ghost. It's the barely perceptible note made by the snapping of spider silk. The sun stolen from your heart by a thief in the twilight.

desperation

Apparently a Desperado is a bottle of beer with a tequila shot, so that is much more fun than desperation, consume with moderation please.

Is Des-peration anything to do with Des O'Connor, apologies to our younger viewers? Or is it anything to do with perspiration, or des-perspiration? Should we just swat this one out?

Desperation is the low point before we turn things around, sink or swim. Desper? A lack of hope? The light at the end of the tunnel, hopefully.

The term was maybe coined in New York City, where people were using it by the 1830s to describe the original town at the southern tip of Manhattan. As New York grew into a city, the only way it could get bigger was by growing to the north, like a plant will grow towards the light. The 'up' and 'down' came from the maps of the time in which up was north and down was south. However, it was not included in dictionaries as late as the 1880s.

But just 20 years later, in the 1900s, the term had been adopted by cities all across the United States and Canada to refer to the historical heart of the city, which coincidentally, was very often the same as the commercial heart of the city.

energy (1)

She's stumbling at the back, red faced and lagging, the bald commando shouts toxic encouragements with no sweat.

Noxious air bites on her dry throat, thick with CO_2 and other mixtures. She suspects he is hating her, that he wants to sprint up front with all the athletes, but stuck at the back he pleasures himself at her failing efforts.

"It's just a jump to the left!"

"Oh sweet Jesus, not yet!"

Zach Seklof groped for the snooze button on the uni-wand by his bed like a newly born kitten. Theoretically sentient yet clinically unable, as yet, to open his eyes. That holo-alarm had seemed like such a hoot when Flo had given it to him for Christmas but in the elemental darkness of a January morn after a night on the Fullers having Tim Curry doing a virtual grind in your direction is none too pretty. Flo remained oblivious. Flo often did. It's a talent.

"Oh merde!" His mood was not improved by the discovery that he had invoked that 10-minute escape clause more times than he had thought. Better call in and make some excuses in advance.

"Call Spectrum!"

"DIALLING... CONNECTED."

"Spectrum, Chris speaking."

"Oh hi Chris, running a bit late today..." opened Seklof weakly.

"Heard it! You know the drill, Zachery. Get your arse down here and get on with it. You know the alternative..."

"OK, OK! I'll be there in 20 minutes!"

"CEASE."

"DISENGAGING... CALL CEASED."

"Fucking bicycle repair man. Bloody toady like the rest of 'em."

Zach lycra'd up and popped open a tin of Willesden Green. What he would have given for the bacon and eggs of his youth. Of course since the food shortages of the '20s, BritGov had resorted to doling out tins of a pâté-like substance named simply after its colour and place of manufacture. Most people reckoned it tasted of, well, Willesden.

He pushed off and joined the insectoid throng of London Road swarming towards the Spectrum power mill.

"Another day at La Bastille."

Chris was there at his position already as Zach shuffled into the dynamo room, Bulbous and leering like a slave ship drummer. Eleven other bodies were already toiling away, one position stood idle. It had his name on it, blinking red on the LCD screen facing him. Chris sniggered.

"Let's see some action, Seklof! Get pumping! Mayor Beckham wants to see the lights on today!"

It was fear more than duty that carried him onto the bike. Slowly gathering pace his limbs were crying out already. Sixty-seven. Another eight years before they'd let him stop. He had not noticed that his legs were not moving until they hauled him away, tears but no weeping, as he briefly recalled another life.

"Lights... LIGHTS!"

Flo sat alone in the darkness, feebly wafting the uni-wand at the silent EntCube.

extremism (1)

Ninety miles an hour downhill towards a sheer drop. Blood pumping and teeth clenched in anticipation of beating the best. The rush.

Commitment is everything, freedom of movement, chasing a thrill. There is no other way, no other life. Just this and now. The cuts, bumps, cracks and tears. Signs of devotion.

Faith marked large by this holy mission, this pilgrimage of pain.

'Twas as good as silent, the passage cross the river that night. Faith I must tell thee that my sculling may just as well have stirred the devil from his very moorings what with the hubbub I had left in my wake. And I tell thee an'all Old Nick would have settled himself right in as though snug in his favoured tavern that evening. Aye, right at home. And I would have joined him in his cups as soon you like. My gizzard fair rasping! I would have traded my safe passage for a single tankard in Ye Olde Black Swan, I say.

Nay, sir, you could not picture the sight. None you say would suffice. The flames fair touched the moon. The reek of powder! My adventures in the Low Countries do not match it. Troopers running pell-mell like rats with their arse on fire. Like I say! Some of them did! Heathens all. I think none of it.

Did we do right? Faith I cannot say. The die is cast and I have little sorrow oer't. For my part I struck the match and ran like stink fair pissing myself as I went. I will not say I have not thought these past days "Oh, Guido, what hath thee achieved save slaughter?"

'Tis done. The common folk will think o'it as they will. There may come a time when the name of Guido Fawkes shall be known to man and child alike. The people shall light fires in my name on this day. Aye, they'll not forget me. Drink up, sir! I'll stand thee another!

fashion

The ultimate in self-expression, fashion forms and is formed by the reflection of the urban population's desire to be ever-changing chameleons in matters of style, food, design of buildings, art and clothing.

Fashion is defined by the dictates of the city dwellers, ever tiring of the status quo, and desirous above all of appearing to be all knowing and in possession of withheld information, hiding and being, give birth to the vestiges of urban power.

She found herself running down the middle of the road. She was wearing a white nightshirt and no shoes. Her long blonde hair streamed out behind her. Her feet were grass-stained and there was a purple-black bruise circling each of her wrists like a bangle. Just like in a dream she had arrived at the place without knowing how she had got there. The overriding feeling was of suffocation. The night was dark, scarcely a star. She saw the dotted white lines in the middle of the road stretch out in front of her and with nowhere else to go followed them in an imprecise sprint.

Up ahead she could just make out a blurry figure in black. A cat miaowed. She could hear it, but not see it. It miaowed again. Plaintive and insistent, however she kept on running. She didn't want to go towards the figure, to make it any clearer, but was drawn ever forwards, the vague and indistinct memory of what was behind tightening in her chest like a corset that is being pulled too tight. Did she ever wear a corset? She wasn't sure, it didn't seem like the kind of thing she would have been allowed to wear, as it would have given her the freedom to display her curvaceousness in a way that, she had a vague memory, would have been frowned upon.

The tarmac hurt her feet. She remembered from a science class many years ago that the first known city to have its streets paved with tar was Baghdad in the eighth century AD. Tarmac (short for tarmacadam, or tar-penetration macadam) refers to a material patented by Edgar Purnell Hooley in 1901; a mechanical mixture of tar and aggregate which was compacted with a steam-roller. She couldn't believe she was thinking of that now, in this place — wherever she was, but the mind was prone to flights of fancy and spewing out its useless ephemera when threatened.

She was now getting closer, and it was closer. A hooded figure. A hoody figure? She stopped. A growing dread of what she might see, who this might be in this dark, deserted street. Her heart beating faster and faster, thumping so hard, she thought she would be sick right there. And the figure has sensed that she is there, or maybe it had watched her desperate flight all along but made no offer of help. And *she/he/it* was turning, but slowly, as if the world had shifted so that every millisecond took a second, and every second took a minute, and every minute took an hour. And now she was now face to face. Face to face with the thing.

A sacred day, well planned and meant. Attended by people they hardly know and eating food that neither liked, but keeping happy. Panicked rush, stilted conversations, put the music on and prevent too much or it might get ugly, these people aren't a natural mix, they should be kept in separate rooms. Discomfort blue, borrowed ideas and everyone says it was so nice, but keeping happy and hoping it will end soon.

Of course that's never it, plenty left and a few more snaps, some speeches and paper thrown in hair. A dance and buffet, soft light and cutting cakes; awkward silence over cheap Champagne, but keeping happy, as they'll be paying for it with the rest of their lives.

I found it in my purse, scrabbling about for the coins to get enough to get over to the next town, cos L was going to give me some money owed me if I could meet him at The Three Pigeons, and I was pretty skint that month.

Three 10ps, four 20ps and six 5ps. Though when I arranged them in a neat line according to their size and denomination, I noticed one of the 5ps was distinctly thinner than the others. On closer inspection, I discovered it to be a dime.

On a chest of drawers in the bedroom lies a pile of coins from other countries of the approximate sizes of those from the UK, collected up from change slipped into hands, into pockets, or purse, along with the remnants carried back from those rare foreign holidays, places one day perhaps to be revisited, perhaps not, for who knows what reasons.

I give the coins to the driver, the dime buried in the middle of its silvery cousins, hoping that he won't have the time to look properly. It's the last money in my purse till Giro-day, unless I can meet up with L. The driver drops the dime in with the other money and gives me my ticket.

And this coin, originally minted an ocean away, carries on its intercontinental journey, to be passed into the hands of another unsuspecting courier, to end up in a foreign coin pile on a chest of drawers, who knows where.

Will these coins ever make it back to their place of origin, or like me, wander far from home, never staying long in the place they were minted?

And I get off at the next town, and continue my journey.

Someone had already decided, but they asked him anyway. It didn't really make any sense, but then nothing any of these people said ever did. If it makes them happy then well, whatever?

But he'd rather be kicking a ball or having a drink, or something.

friendship

As you get older you find you have less of it.

gentrification

Representatives of missing Putney man Mr William Benn have announced today that an application has been made to the High Court to have Mr Benn legally declared deceased.

Mr Benn, a reclusive former bank employee, had lived close to the river at number 52 Festive Road for 'at least 40 years' according to local sources, but has not been seen entering or leaving the property since 2005. He would now be 73 years of age.

His friend, and long time business associate Mr Frederick 'Smasher' Lagru, who is making the application, had this to say today: "Bill was my friend, I shall miss him terribly, but as the years pass any hope I had of seeing him again has gone I'm afraid. Those few of us that knew him must move on and settle his estate without any further ado". He also claimed that a memorial paving stone will be set outside his house to honour Mr Benn's passing.

The announcement has though, been met with criticism by other members of Mr Benn's social circle. Local shopkeeper Mr Ferris 'Fez' Cooper, who has vowed to challenge any ruling, had this to say regarding today's events: "Bill will be back, you mark my words. He was always going off when he was younger. He used to tell me such tales over a pint down The Duke's Head. Lagru's after the house, you mark my words. It's fishy this is."

Mr Lagru has not yet revealed whether Mr Benn has made a will of any sort. Showing our reporter round the house today Lagru pointed out some of the more unusual items amongst Benn's few belongings. They include a pirate flag, a sheriff's badge, and even a stone hammer, though little of any value. It is though, the house, that is likely to become a bone of contention amongst Mr Benn's few confidantes.

52 Festive Road is estimated to be worth as much as £800,000 on the open market. Mr Cooper remarked to our reporter at the end of the interview that the house had been bought by Mr Benn for as little as £6,000 in the 1960s. "There's more than one killing that Lagru's making today, that's for sure. I shall contest this," continued Cooper. And with that he was gone. *The Times* will bring you more on this story as it unfolds.

Obituary — William Benn — 1940-2013, page 32.

glow

Have you ever noticed how it never really gets dark anymore? Even during the putative earth daytime we shun elemental light for the delights of toiling away in halogen dungeons getting pixel burn on the back of our retinas.

Of course one of the primary facets of addiction is that one can never see it in oneself. It has become second nature to stagger blinking from our cells peering at the backlit screen that we have not had the nerve to peek at for the last four hours. Scurrying forth in search of buses permanently illuminated inside and out for fear of litigation. Or down holes in the ground similarly fitted out for very similar reasons.

Red-eyed and fevered, we stumble home and fumble, reach for the switch, pull the cord, turn the dial. Made uneasy by silence, by stillness, but most of all, by darkness.

We have, since birth, been taught to fear true elemental darkness. It is a species' memory that we simply cannot erase. It is this primal dread that created the spark that created the fire we once clustered around. Not without reason in truth, beasts once lurked in the woods of England and still do, of a sort, in its alleyways.

But that's not it, is it? As children we feared the thing under the bed would get us once the switch was flicked but we are children no more, surely? The monsters are all banished back into our imagination. All we have to fear in the night is our own reflection and that is our collective terror. We fear being alone in our own heads. It's why we need our hit.

But it hurts, doesn't it? This eternal monochrome.

It varies in its intensity but you couldn't call it light. It's as though the states of light and darkness have reached some form of negotiated peace brokered by phosphorescent middle men. We have merely negated a negation.

Don't your eyes hurt? So tired, aren't you? We are slowly losing our circadian perspective.

That thing in the sky is no lily to be eternally gilded in its presence then replicated when it leaves us. So we have attained the power to negate the heavens. Masters of the universe. But we have lost our anchors, our objects. It is no easy thing to face the day when one no longer knows where it begins and ends.

From a distance it all looks so beautiful. A bowl of precious gems sparkle on the horizon. Strings of pearls beckon us to follow them like breadcrumbs out of the forest to safety. If only we had known. It's just not worth it. The raised blood pressure. The muscle spasms. The increased risk of cancer. The sagging cheekbones. Switch it all off, why don't you? Watch the LEDs die away and exhale. Just close your eyes and accept that we all sleep alone. You'll feel better in the morning.

What was that noise? Oh, trust me, it's probably nothing.

Blue?
Jus' blue?

There. Blue.
Blue like just before it turns into night…
…Blue like the wings of a dragonfly…
Dancing delicately in the sun.

Nah… sparkling like gold… like a ring round the
finger… Bling.

Azure…
Like the sea in the Med…

Burgundy. Like the bottle of port dad thinks he's got
hidden for Christmas.
Bloody, thickly, stickly, sweet,
Dribblesome.

…White — white, like thick snow when it settles…
Or grey like when you jump and jump on the snow,
and it melts and mushes.

Cherry. Red. Ripe. Juicy.

Green — like the grass under the upturned
wheelbarrow that hasn't
darkened.

Violet like…
Violet…Vio… Violette... Viola... Violent…

I can paint a rainbow.

haven

It was another golden morning in the high 'Burbs, deep in the North Downs. The sort that great green effervescing Surrey Oaks wait out the winter for. This is their big moment and they do not disappoint, thought Manny as he whistled his way along Church Lane.

As he approached the wrought iron gates of number 40 an arthritic rough collie that he knew to be called Ding, (the 'o' is silent), waddled into view making a half-arsed attempt to assert his authority. As usual he gave up half way down the drive as Mrs O'Conner opened the front door to him while simultaneously hauling a shocking pink robe towards decency and not quite achieving it.

"Morning, Manny, anything for me?"

"No, missus, I just come to look at you and say hi to Ding."

"Oh, shut up and hand it over! Time for a brew, young man?"

"Fraid not this time, the boss is getting fed up of us getting back late. And if you're an agency boy they can get rid of you real easy, and I ain't a vet yet, I need the dough. 'Sides I'd miss the pair of you!"

"Oh stop it! You tell that Micky Temple he'll have

me to deal with if he does! Well, see you Monday then, bye-ee!" And with that off she flounced back inside.

"One of these days," chuckled Manny to himself as he shut the gate behind him.

Meanwhile at 42 'The Haven', behind a wall of barely legal Leylandii, curtains are twitching.

"He's ruddy late again, Irene! Why can't we have Bryan back like we used to! That African chap can't be bothered, thinks he's too good to be a postie, he should feel bloody lucky...."

In the corner the *Daily Mail* rustled and responded: "Bryan was made redundant six months ago, dear. He wasn't any quicker than the new chap. He told me they were making the rounds..."

"That's not the point, Irene! We knew him. We could trust him. We both watched that documentary. Nicking ruddy credit cards they were."

"That was in London, Gerald dear...."

Outside, Manny negotiated the towering oak gate framed in the giant hedge. There was a knack to it. Its great weight had caused it to sag on its hinges and Manny could only move it by shouldering it off the ground, scuffing gravel hither and thither as he did so.

After delivering the assorted adverts and offers through the letterbox he repeated the process almost identically in reverse. Almost.

Three things then happened at virtually the same time, two of which were most unfortunate.

Firstly, Manny wheeled away down Church Lane feeling good in the sunshine. Secondly, said huge hunk of timber wheezed and sagged off its latch, settling a good three inches back into the drive. Thirdly, two put-upon self-entitled knuckles tightened around a net curtain.

Around an hour after these events a rather wind-blown Manny freewheeled into the delivery office yard and parked up. It had been a good day. Not late and no returns to explain to Micky. Time to toss the bag and pick up his ride home. He was just about to meet up with the guys when he noticed the toad-like figure of Micky gesturing to join him in his glass box.

"You've bin a naughty boy, int ya? I've bin 'earing about you."

Then the overly familiar clasp around the shoulders. The kiss (goodbye) of death before you go down the road. To his credit Manny shrugged him off pretty quick and shot him a few choice words in Yoruban, but it matters none at this point. Time to hand in their bike and get on yours.

A couple of the other Nigerian lads did some posturing but they knew the score. They liked him but not more than next week's money. And so, you might think, that was that, but unfortunate events have a habit of biting their originator on the arse.

Come Monday it became apparent to the regular troops that there was a Manny-shaped hole on the bench for walk 35. This was discussed in the usual way by its neighbouring custodians. By shouting and swearing a lot.

"I 'eard it with me own ears, Trig."

"Well oo else's ears would you use, Deano? Mind, if I 'ad ears like yours I'd use some other fucker's..."

"Language, Toby."

"Bollocks, Flossy."

"What's that, Toby?"

"It's English, Trig. You should try it some time."

"Trig, that dick'ead from Church Lane rang up about the casual lad. Made some shit up about breakin 'is garden gnome. 'E said I broke 'is letterbox last year."

"You did."

"That ain't the point. It was an accident."

"You kicked it."

"Fuck off."

"Lads, lads, I think what young Deano is grasping for is a plan of action regarding Mr Leadbetter at number 42. He's reported all of us at one time or another. Only difference is we don't care, cos Mickey can't sack us. Now he's got one of our boys..."

"He was a casual..."

"...ahem, shush, Floss, OUR BOYS, sacked."

"Well then..."

"Well then..."

On Tuesday morning Gerald Leadbetter groaned the groan of a fifty-something executive picking up the mail. For some reason it was all muddy despite the dry weather. At least it looked like mud.

He dismissed it from his mind and hurried from the house to make the 7.32am to Waterloo...

"What the ruddy hell...?"

"He'll never get it open."

"How many of these sodding things are there?!!"

"'Bout 500, wasn't it, Floss?"

"Exactly 500, Trig."

"He could get it open with a sharp knife."

"After a while, Tobes. He ain't getting that train that's for sure."

"Thirsty, Deano?"

"Let's get out of 'ere, Trig, before someone sees us. The Richmond it is."

And so our heroes rode away into the drizzly sunrise to drink to absent friends and steam in front of the fire. Gerald Leadbetter got the tie-wraps off. Eventually. He got to work three hours late and was not fired.

There are historically three ways that a human may achieve altitude in the built environment above London. These may be said to be both corporeal and symbolic.

Horatio Nelson, for instance, dwells in a sarcophagus in St Paul's Cathedral, yet his 18ft likeness glowers imperiously above Trafalgar Square atop 150ft of granite. Put on his pedestal at the cost of a grateful nation to survey the city with cold unrealistic eyes encrusted with pigeon guano. The dead hero's dandruff.

His monument has also suffered the indignities of parachuting protesters, phony sales to gullible Americans and even John Noakes. But the man himself suffers no more.

Anthony Gormley placed 31 exact bronze likenesses of himself across the South Bank skyline at the behest of an enthralled municipality. The purpose of the installation was, in his words, 'to get under people's skin' and make you 'feel slightly uncertain about what's going on in the world that you are living in'.

The artist's presence is projected across urban space, yet he remains unseen. He places himself subliminally in the city's consciousness. He has to a degree achieved the same elevation as Nelson without dying. Mind you, he never got to fight sea battles and have a racy ménage à trois with Lady Hamilton and her doddery old husband either. Them's the breaks. The statues were often mistaken for potential suicides.

A third way is to become entombed in a snot and plastic sarcophagus on the twentieth floor of Michael Cliffe House listening to the wind rattle the windows, sometimes ripping them from their hinges. It has since its '60s construction as a phallic projection of Finsbury style hubris, invited at least 20 souls to (briefly) have total certainty about the world they have lived in.

And those who remain? They also have certainty of a sort. For some people, to know that tomorrow will be just like today is a source of comfort. For most council block dwellers it seems to be a source of nervousness. Ontological security can be a curious thing.

The first two examples are symbolic in nature, a tangible projection of an absent original cast from collective and personal hubris.

The third is the corporeal lived experience of the victims of somebody else's.

high street

She teeters over cobbled stones in shoes unsuitable
for movement, checking the walls are still real,
not trusting two centuries of concrete on a night
like this, she hopes it's all another dream. The
throbbing head and wine stained teeth, chewing
wet lettuce on unspecific meat, accompanied by a
piss sweat stench. Right now she's the queen of the
town.

hive (1)

They swarmed round her on set. She didn't have a moment to herself. An actress who would not live long in life, but whose films would make her live forever.

hive (2)

Flustered walkers clustered in hope of a solution,
if they keep bustling, jostling and huddling
something will sort itself out. The walk to nowhere
must go somewhere, but probably ends up where
it began, keeping pace with the apparition beside
that makes you feel closer and makes you stick.

homeless

It wasn't meant to be there, but added something inexplicable to the character of the square. It was ugly and served no purpose. It made people uncomfortable and ask questions of themselves they would rather not be asked. On hot days it got in the way as it spread across the path and rested itself on railings. It left its business behind a tree. The people said it had been there for a good long time, but that they just tried to ignore it. It was true.

identity

You are advised to set your password to something unguessable.

industry

A Promethean saviour, proclaimed by virgin
leaders to strip away the wasted labour. Growth
through starvation, mixed with kind words,
encouraging the whipped dog to save its fickle
master. And yet the dog looks kindly back and
licks his master's feet. We rush to fight the threat,
which looks to prove the git correct. When told no,
or it cannot be done, a choice to sit and scorn seems
unlikely.

Over the pond, it becomes a weapon of choice,
yet here is met with ridicule.

Impossibility our trade, we thrive on something
out of nothing — creative minds and broken backs
wear welts of pride.

My husband leaves a message on my mobile saying I need to get out of Gillingham on Saturday but doesn't say why.

I imagine radioactive goo pouring through the streets of Medway. An earthquake. The Return of the Ents.

Nope, it's just the Gillingham Gills. Up against rival Swindon.

Apparently there was some rowdiness at the last game.

An initiative is set: more police (lots more police) or the game goes on with the bleachers empty. And this is how living on Priestfield Road becomes a Zen koan: if Gillingham plays Swindon and no one comes to see it, is there really a football game?

invisible

I saw an attractive young man, head bowed, fringe covering his face like a curtain, stooping, tentative gait. The teenage girls sat giggling, not even noticing as he passed by. He was quite overweight.

When you are fat, you have a disguise. If you are only slightly overweight they can still see you. They can giggle and whisper, so you eat more.

Obesity makes you disappear into yourself and lets you hide from them.

It seemed as though it had been raining for days. Perhaps it had, Gert mused to herself as she tucked into a bit of Red on potato bread. First a famine, now a flood, whatever next?

She dressed carefully, the doc might be a looker after all. All the time hacking profusely. She sat back heavily on the bed and clocked herself in the mirror, checking her ambitions on that score. Grilled spam ain't an attractive skin tone.

The Parkway was deserted as she made her way to the bus stop. Gert hugged herself against a lazy wind that fluttered the polythene in the trees. Presently the D11 appeared to convey her to the health centre.

When Gert was a child these machines had drivers. Now, when there were no other passengers she thought it surreal to trundle past swings and roundabouts as though on a plastic barge floating along at Alton Towers. When had she last seen water that wasn't falling from the sky? Even the peddlers weren't out in this.

At last the greige bunker that is the Kingsway Oxfam Clinic[1] hove into view. Spattered by rain and starlings it had developed the same patina as an old smoker's face. In the same way that tins of salmon used to display a picture of a fish on the side.

Gert shouldered her way past the masked security guards resplendent in their Kevlar vests to punch in her arrival at the console. It flickered slightly as she did so.

"Lazy fuckers not peddling hard enough," she wheezed in the narrow space still available under her breath.

The waiting area was curiously quiet, still, on such an apocalyptic day perhaps even the sick had thought better of dragging their bones through the borderland.

After a short while leafing through the purple pages of one of the incest weeklies a digitised mid-Atlantic voice cracked the musty silence.

"MISS LUSCH — PROCEED TO SURGERY 3. YOU HAVE TEN MINUTES," as a wall mounted timer began to descend.

The doctor was verging on the elderly with quite a kind face, Gert thought. Gert had thought a lot today. There hadn't been anyone to talk to. For some reason she didn't understand he was wearing full surgical garb.

"Good morning, Miss Lusch. My name is Dr Friend. Please have a seat."

Gert assumed the position and began to reel off the usual array of 'flu-related ailments which could mean either a sniffle or death.

"It's got a lot worse than when I was here last week..."

Her words fell away as it occurred to her that Dr Friend was not even registering that she was speaking. He was shaking a little though. All soaks the bloody lot of them.

"I have the results of your genetic testing, Miss Lusch," he interrupted, a little rudely in Gert's opinion.

"...I'm afraid it is my duty to inform you that you have a chance greater than 65% of developing a malignancy within the next five years thus compromising your future economic viability..."

"I'm what?"

"...It is therefore also my duty to further inform you that under the powers of the Public Health Act of 2017 that you be removed from your estate..."

"But..."

"...to a place of secure exclusion."

"Basil will be home at five!"

"You will in due course be granted your statutory right to a government appointed second opinion. I'm very sorry, Miss Lusch."

Two sturdy shadows fell across surgery 3 as the D11 trundled past the bars of the window.

"MISS LUSCH, YOUR TIME IS UP."

[1] *Since the reforms instituted by the then Health Secretary Nigella Lawson, in 2016/17, all medical provision outside the private sector has been exclusively provided by charitable organisations.*

isolation (2)

The seams between the cupboard walls transmit no
light into my tiny room. Sweat droplets sooth my
heated skin as I lose my balance, brushing against
the sides and right myself, reminded of the fall.
He put it up high, above the musty place and no
way my feet will touch the ground this time. So
I'm perched, claws out waiting for release, but then
there is a sound. He thinks too much about what's
happening here, when he could take a look and
feed me for a change. Does he think I've got
something going on in here? Is there a party or
does he just suspect I know the way out?

jersey-strip

Our arteries are becoming clogged by primary
coloured plastic. The bypass needs a bypass. These
umbilici, coursing with blood and guts to the
gyring hub which pisses fatigue and cynicism back
out at us, structurally excludes the pedestrian. It
repulses bipeds.

Islands of humanity atrophy as the tourniquet
tightens its grip. As time and traffic pass, once
pearly nets darken imperceptibly until greasy grey.
They become as one with UPVC frames that only
ever looked new in the showroom. Eventually,
overnight, they calcify into brown metal shutters.

Twenty years of diesel monsters, hooting
German jalopies, and gurning plasterers gobbing
their greetings takes its toll. Rather than repopulate
these places the planners tend to just hide them
behind wheezing non-specific evergreens until the
inevitable change of use notice is posted on the
nearest telegraph pole.

Home by home, unit by unit, the negation of the
non-commercial becomes complete. Homo-
economicus are bussed in from Barrett-Land to
stops where the pavement ends 20ft either side.

Thus the impossibility of walking becomes
complete.

kaleidoscope

She was strapped into the contraption at the
Memory Recognition Institute. Her head was
surrounded by hard white plastic, moulded to
each individual's shape. This was the famous
'Brain Pillow', invented by researchers early in the
twenty-first. Initially used to help people recover
their memories after serious brain trauma, the team
of Memmers were the only ones now allowed to
enter the machines, in search of disobedience.

The device was turned on; to the Seers a faint
blue glow around her head indicated all was
working properly.

For as long as she could remember this had
been her life. Enter the machine. Enter the
collective consciousness. She knew everything
about everybody. Only the other Memmers and the
Seers knew anything about her. It was sometimes
hard to look another Memmer in the eye, once you
had been in their head.

At least, they knew the facts, but not the thoughts.
Right now she thought, were it not for them and
the white plastic she might as well not exist. The
old man had really got to her.

She had no idea how old he had been – that's

the trouble they didn't anticipate with the Green. Nobody seemed to know exactly what it was made of, but on certain individuals it had an unexpected result of prolonging life indefinitely.

They had asked her to go into his head, this ancient, frail being — what could he have done that was so wrong? Every memory of everything he'd ever done or ever seen stored in his brain, like on the hard drive of a computer, and it had all been still there, waiting to be accessed. But something was different this time. She had a vague memory of once doing something, nothing particularly memorable, but it started unrelated memories popping into her head. Cycling past a cornfield on a sunny day, Flo turning and laughing at something when she was young and beautiful, an evening I was out walking the dog with my dad and the moon was so close it looked like you could reach your arm out and touch it...

In the Memory Recognition Institute, Seer #862-Y looked up from his portable display, surprise on his face.

The gates of the park were shut when we got there. Our dog called Ben who was the first dog called Ben, though over the years there were two more, but he was the original and best, wanted to go for a run in the park, so my dad lifted him over the wall, which was only knee-high. He lifted me over and climbed over himself. He let Ben off the lead.

Seer #862-Y called for his supervisor, Seer #132-A+. They both stood transfixed, had never seen this before, did not know what to do, as Memmer Second Class Carmina Tatangelo, Mina, was surrounded by a mist of whirling colours, as she dreamed another man's memories.

The machine was turned off, the alarms rang, but Mina did not awaken.

The woman in the bank explained it all to me. About how my *behavioural wheel* had a number of red patches around the rim.

It was because I did not have any insurance. It was because I had not made a will. Having extracted from me during her expertly polished patter the fact that I have a son, she pointed out that such things were *important*.

I replied to her that I did not have anything to insure, and that being the case, that I had nothing that I could leave. I do not for instance, even own a *house* in which to put such notional riches.

She smiled at me that smile that is only ever witnessed in these palaces of financial services or in an Olympic pool during the synchronised swimming.

Raising one immaculately pencilled brow she intimated that within 'a few years' a *State* pension will not be an option for a sensible person... she left a silence for this earth shattering knowledge to sink in. And, in the future I *may* own a house...

The future. Both she and I know that unless the words that you are reading are one day discussed by Kirsty Wark on BBC2 I am unlikely to have what the English apparently dream of as soon as weaned.

A castle in the sky. To put all those *things* in. Those things that matter so much to the synchronised splashers in the sharkpool. And the ones that want to be them. She is talking again, but all I can hear are the ominous cellos of austerity.

kudos

You will respect me
Got Hackett on my jacket
Shiver in the cold

light

It floats in the atmosphere,

~~obscuring~~

the

*

st   rs.

loneliness

Is a cowboy without any shoes, riding a three-legged horse to a nameless town, by a river that runs nowhere.

It had taken Flo quite some time to get out of the apartment. The central locking system had fused all the doors shut when the power was cut. And it *had* been cut. She had dismissed the darkness initially as one of the periodic shutdowns experienced by the good folk of A3Burb when the peddlers had been thinned during the holwindow.

Clearly this was not about a lack of leg power in general. Outside The Fugue the grid got thinner for sure but she could hear the trams were running and even Zach would have made it home by now. Besides, he would have called. He always called. If he knew what was good for him. No. The power was off on purpose. They had shared the light for decades and now they were being made to share the darkness too.

Well, so be it. Magnetic locks are no match for a meat tenderiser wielded by a disgruntled Aberdonian. Flo's hair was decorated with a few splinters and smoked slightly as she trudged up Green Lanes to see a certain gentleman. It looked quite becoming in the moonlight but it would have taken a brave chap to have pointed that out under the circumstances.

Green Lanes is known to the whole neighbourhood as a place for the obtaining of the illicit. It led to an abandoned part of town known simply as 'Down'. It was rumoured that people still lived in there although that may have been to stop teenagers from hanging out beyond parental control. Judging by the standard of the graffiti[1] it occurred to Flo that that gambit had clearly failed.

So much for what 'everyone' knew about Down. A thing that hardly anyone knew was that deep in the undergrowth, virtually engulfed by ivy, was a telephone kiosk. This in itself was unusual as they had ceased to exist in most of the nation years since. What made this one unique was that it actually still worked. Flo had to use all her might to shoulder the door open wide enough to get through. The original keypad had been replaced by a single button that bore the number 42 on it.

"Fuckin' little nerd," said Flo under her breath as she lifted the handset and pressed it.

"I haird thait," replied an exaggeratedly cultured Scottish accent. It was just like Flo's only different.

"Lerrus in, Ja, I'm gasping for drink and a sit down."

"Password please, if you will. And the name's Jazdy. Prawo Jazdy."

"Fuckin ell, whatever. ARTHUR DENT! Now open the ruddy door!"

"As you will."

With that the side of the kiosk slid open and a small hairy man in a plaid shirt beckoned her to follow.

Flo seated herself in an old wicker chair while 'Prawo' stooped over the fridge to select some beverages. The room was made completely of glass and was utterly surrounded by foliage.

"So lady, to what do I owe this pleasure?"

Flo then launched into her tale of woe regarding the power in the apartment, Zach vanishing and the refusal of her tram pass on the D14. As she continued Prawo's face fell by the minute.

"I'm sure he'll turn up," he replied with little conviction. "What do you need me for?"

"I need to get into The City. You can lie to me all night but I know that's where those bastards have taken him."

Mr Jazdy (for now) took the short journey of rising to his full height and walked over to an antique Bisley filing cabinet next to the fridge. After rummaging for a moment he drew out a familiar blue card with the familiar swoosh symbol on the front.

"Take this for all the good it'll do ya. Good luck and you've never heard of me."

"Are you sure this'll work? They're all persona... THIS IS FUCKIN' MINE, YOU LITTLE RATBAG!"

"*Like* yours, but not the original. It will work though. Take it or leave it."

Flo finished her beer and silently nodded her gratitude. As she moved towards the door she turned as curiosity got the better of her.

"Why *Prawo Jazdy?*"

"It was expedient for me to do so for my current purposes. Be lucky and give him my regards if you ever find him."

"You're all heart."

A light silty drizzle knocked the last of the masonry from Flo's hair as she emerged from the jungle and turned towards town. It tap-danced on the newly minted Mr Jazdy's roof as his knuckles whitened on the arms of his chair, eyes tightly shut but angled at the heavens.

[1]*Under the so-called 'Goldpeg' laws adopted in the early '20s under the then Home Secretary Mr Lewisohn, graffiti was legal if the property's owner hadn't applied for an exemption certificate. Still rigorously censored, it was seen as a more harmless form of self expression than that printed on a page.*

metropolis

Metro? The Metro is the funkiest underground system in the whole world! It always smells of stink bombs, and no one cares if you jump over the barriers, even though the tickets cost next to nothing. Just because you can thumb your nose at the system. The posters on the rounded, white-tiled walls are lacking in imagination and purely for information. However — and this is the coolest — you can actually use your mobile in the train as the tunnels are so close to the surface of Paris.

Polis? Police? Urban police, country police? The term polis, which in archaic Greece meant city, changed with the development of the governance centre in the city to indicate state, and finally with the emergence of a citizenship notion between the land owners it came to describe the entire body of citizens. So my definition of metropolis is all the people who travel in the Metro, those lucky tikes!

metropolitan

1. Fill the shaker 2/3 full of icy demeanours;

2. Add the alcoholic mixture of brandy and vermouth fumes and mix until really bitter;

3. Make sure the shaker is tightly secured then shake vigorously for 30 minutes;

4. The contents should then be well strained through the gates of Wembley Central;

5. Garnish with a surprising squeeze of melon;

6. Pour out (your heart) immediately (when you get home).

migration

Caged pigeons can't fly south since they ate the
bread from cities. I think the tall buildings confuse
them. Lured by the smell of rotting decadence,
thrown to the kerb, they find themselves entranced
by reflected surfaces, never realising that their
wings have been clipped.

multicultural

A selection of bacteria fight for survival at the bottom of a small glass jar. Spreading patterns of birth and decay on the transparent surface they float and fail, fighting for freedom, forced into captivity by a rubber seal. Nothing remains the same and one day they will cure cancer.

neon

Vacancy — Free TV
Grey plaid
White walls
Black top
Polka dot
Cigarette
Gotta light?
Black stockings
White lies
Jim Beam
Margarita
Dollar bill
Juke joint
Red nails
White socks
Baby Doll!
Daddio!
~~Vacancy~~ — Free TV

night bus

A collection of grimacing grotesques swap brightly coloured costumes and fill the space with movement. Parked in a big top and eating something I shouldn't; I begin to feel unwell. The people crowd around and the exit seems distant, blocked and barred. I hide my food and focus on the action. Smoke rises from the floor, they clap and sing. We arrive in Tangier, but I swear we never left our seats.

orbital (1)

Mina awoke twelve days later in a pale green
room. In a bed with a patchwork counterpane.
This was somewhere new in the complex that she
hadn't been taken before. Being a Memmer had a
lot of privileges but she was only Second Class. Or
at least that had been what the initial test score had
said back when she was eleven.

At the Coming of Age rite her parents had been
so proud, when her test score indicated that their
daughter Carmina Tatangelo, who had never
achieved anything of note at Scule, not even in the
monthly imagineering expeditions to the Outside,
had the propensity for the Brain Pillow. From
that day when she was taken away to begin her
training, excused from the daily Scule lessons,
Mina had not seen her parents. But she
remembered they had looked happy. At least that's
what the Head Seer at the time had told all the
children who were removed: "Your parents are
very proud."

At his control desk, Seer #132-A+ was beginning
to think something must have been wrong with
that initial assessment. Could it be that they had
underestimated Mina's latent abilities? They had
never known anything like what happened the last

time Mina was placed in the machine. Some of the colours that orbited around her for the next three days had not been seen for centuries. Had only been passed down in stories. When the colours stopped, still asleep, she was taken out of the machine and bought here, to this lab deep inside the Memory Recognition Institute, to be studied.

For three days the Seers basked in Mina's rainbow glow. They thought for a second to keep it secret, but there are no secrets between Seers.

For twelve days Mina had been scanned and studied and when that revealed nothing they resorted to touching her face with the palm of the hand, an old, half-forgotten magic, something to do with young ones and parentals, explained Head-Seer Granding, as she pulled off her white glove and placed her hand on Mina's cheek the first time. The other Seers gasped.

Head-Seer Granding suffered no ill effects. In fact it might even be said that as she serenely walked away a little flush could be seen in her marble complexion, such as had last been seen who knows how many years ago when she was much younger.

One by one, over the next few days, every Seer visited Mina, placed their palm on her cheek, but still no response. The Seers walked away in a dreamy cloud and Mina slept, not stirring.

On the twelfth day that changed. The white-dressed young Seer who placed his hand on Mina's cheek had never been this deep in the Orbital Centre before.

He was taller than the others, and his blue eyes had not yet begun to fade as would happen with each subsequent visit into the collective consciousness. His black hair was pulled back into a knot at the nape of his neck. His fingers were long. He brushed Mina's cheek lightly, and the machines monitoring her began to show some interest as her eyelids fluttered open.

The attending Seer #132-A+ motioned to the man standing at Mina's bed, who he did not recognise. Unusual, 132-A+ couldn't reach into his mind.

Mina's eyes focused on the counterpane, it reminded her of something. A thin hand resting on the many coloured hexagons, coming into focus. Mina's gaze followed the hand, the arm, the shoulder, and stopped at the face with its blue eyes.

"You're not..."

"Shush," he said.

132-A+ started towards the bed with his testing unit in his hand.

"Er, excuse me, I don't recognise..."

The stranger touched Seer #132-A+ lightly between the eyes. The Seer's face took on a strange hue, a light mauve just under his eyes and he fell to the floor. Mina looked puzzled.

"Come on," said the stranger, holding out his hand. "Do you want to get out of here or not?"

orbital (2)

Mesmerised by spinning vinyl with thin strips of
light fluttering from behind my ears.

over-crowded (1)

Tonight I was coming home from an event in Soho near Wardour Street while chatting on the phone, and when I looked up I found myself in China-town. I thought I was headed towards Oxford Street, but had been walking in the exact opposite direction of where I was supposed to be going, something I still do often in London. Lit up with dozens of red lanterns and a gigantic dragon perfectly backlit high on a wall, it was all I could do to not abort my Victoria Station mission and get lost in the lanterns. I didn't want to be stranded after the last train though, and told myself I could come back, even though it probably wouldn't look quite the same.

Or maybe Chinatown is always that luminous. I don't understand the magic of London yet, but on a few occasions now, walking by myself through the city well after ten, it's palpable. The streets are sort of foggy and misty, it's not cold and not too hot at all — perfect for endless walking. The huge, antique street lamps glow under window boxes of lush green ivy and bright flowers with names unknown to me. Pubgoers mill about in doorways, holding amber-filled glasses, casting occasional, appraising glances at walkersby. Further along, towards the Picadilly tube station, I pass a drag queen with a pancaked face and a black, curly wig. Twenty-something girls wobble down the sidewalk wearing impossibly short dresses and even more impossible heels. It's near midnight on a Tuesday, but people seem immune to sleep.

OK. I could fall in love with this city.

over-crowded (2)

There is a sensuality in being broken down, the
waters retreat,
return, swallow up, disgorge their
gifts; laid down long ago and forgotten;
mercury, methanol, hydrochloric acid,
formaldehyde, uranium, lead,
radium. They bring a glow,
down to the roots,
10,000 feet beneath the ancestors.
I'm sorry, did you forget something?
There's enough to go around, of course;
no-one goes without.

Frack me 18 times and
move on. Oh methane, this is
not going to end well —
you take my breath away,
disturb my mind,
I lose my touch.
We simply do not mix,
and the dregs of our love
burn me away.

There isn't enough room for us;
one of us must go.

*Hydraulic fracturing, or 'fracking', is the process of drilling
and injecting fluid into the ground at a high pressure in order
to fracture shale rocks to release natural gas inside.*

panopticon

It is not generally possible to hear our guardians at their work down at street level. Sometimes, on a quiet night in the middle of the week the lonely stroller may sense a metallic high pitched whine accompanying their movements, reminiscent of power windows in luxury car ads. It emanates from one of the eyes in the sky that look down upon the central drag of just about everywhere. STNLs© appear to be disproportionately fond of such trinkets.

From long years past the local rags that cover such upwardly mobile satellites, along with their more recent sisterly free sheets, have been offering a weekly fix of prosaic true crime being swatted by the regional bluebottles. The enemy is always at your (electronically controlled) gates, dear people of the shires. But sleep safe, a PC Keen's on the case. Hence the current proliferation of steel spiked snoopers keeping the pigeons company, of which the borough is of course quite rightly proud.

If you do find yourself looking skywards sensing a realignment, don't worry too much. It probably isn't watching you. It is of course not watching anything. It is being operated by two bored council employed kestrels, most likely called Wayne and

Les, although we have no way of knowing that. They are more interested in people moving too fast, moving too slow, wearing a hoodie, hanging around in groups, walking alone. All those recognised markers of a delinquent personality. Just as likely,'probably Wayne' has just decided to home in on any available amount of Lycra-clad gooseflesh quivering on its way into the club, as you pass them by. Norman Bates with a budget. No, not looking at you at all.

But don't you feel safer? I mean, as we've established, it's not watching you, is it? It's them who need to mind what they do. The mutterers and splutterers, the white line walkers, can of Tennent's in one hand, pit bull terrier/Kappa slapper (delete as appropriate) in the other. That's right. No problem then.

Then again, maybe opening that bottle of Wolf Blass in the park wasn't the best move. There's a couple of blue stripe rozzers over there pointing and chatting on their mobiles. Hey, they've walked right past. Lucky escape there. Better not do it again though. Next time might be your turn.

One more simple pleasure constrained.

paranoia

I do not feel safe
When police carry rifles
As I catch my train

pavement

Through the cardboard in my shoes
I can feel you.
Made soft by rain and neon
I am reflected.
After the very last bus
You are my guide.
Tonight the world is ours
And we are joined.

pigeon

The place he took her was encrusted with pigeon guano. She didn't know this area of the city at all. Not Outside, not quite, but not safe within the confines of the few streets that had been her home the past few years either. Many, many years before the event people had lived in these dwellings, made them warm, made them safe, they were now little more than stone windbreaks with an occasional flutter of centuries old curtains still hanging at windows empty of glass.

Every now and then she caught sight of symbols and drawing on the rubble, but she didn't understand the colours, didn't understand what the words meant.

The man had stopped and was looking at a particularly overgrown area with thistles well over his head. 'Bingo!' he said and disappeared. Mina stood there alone, watching the slight rustle. She wondered why she couldn't read him. It gave her a funny feeling, she didn't know who, or what, he was, but she felt perfectly at ease with him.

His head reappeared out of the thistles and he gave her a smile, Mina didn't even know his name, but she felt herself filling with happiness. She shyly smiled back, and he beckoned to her to follow him. As she climbed through the brambles and weeds she couldn't remember feeling this happy in years.

The small glass box was surprisingly still intact, though the roof was almost completely covered with guano and ivy. He pushed at the far wall which slid aside. Once again, she took his hand as she stepped into the unknown.

pollution

A good friend once told me that after using the Bakerloo Line I should blow my nose good and hard whether I needed to or not.

populous

I used to torture the little people on the isometric island, unleashing an earthquake or destroying their houses in fire or by flood. They would swim frantically for a few moments before their pixels disappeared from my screen. I was supposed to lead them to the land of milk and honey, but it was far more fun to fuck with them for a few hours before flicking the thing off and heading to bed.

I haven't played for years, wonder what they're doing?

prostitution

As I made my way through the after-work scrum of Chalk Farm Road I saw her. I tried not to make eye contact but it was too late. She stepped out from the doorway and looked straight at me. They can always make a potential John from 100 yards.

Brazen is the name of this game. She looked stunning from a distance but as she approached the luggage under her pretty brown eyes became apparent. She looked so tired and not a little strung out. How long had she been standing there? I'm always a sucker for a hard luck story and she had me down pat on that score.

I tried to move away, do the speed-up tango, to no avail. Gripping my arm and giving me the fullbeam adoration that should have been saved for something real she just kept talking. Wheedling away at my resistance, flattering my middle aged ego. 'Professionally available' is, I believe, the current euphemism. I knew it was all bullshit but we all love to hear it, right?

Well, to be honest with you guys, just between us, I gave her what she wanted. It had been a while and I have to admit, in the end I wanted it to happen.

So I gave her my details and signed up for a fiver a month. It's all in a good cause right? I must admit though I felt a little used and dirty when she moved on to the next guy.

Don't you see, by this
you are playing right into
Their evil embace?

protest (2)

Lo, and it was written that the firm smack of governance should fall upon the less fashionable postcodes. For they wore hoods, and hung about outside, and did not go to Eton.

But the blow did fail, for it fell upon hard heads and flint hearts sharpened by time and experience. And the blow did recoil upon the aggressor shattering glass all about, bringing forth a death of 1,000 cuts. And new trainers for the neighbourhood.

Wounded, the beast bellowed, "We will teach you the meaning of responsibility!" Out! Out! Begone from your lives of milk and honey! To the streets with you!

Which is where we came in. And those marked with the stigma of sickness grew hardened to their medicine once more and multiplied. And this caused great pain to the shopkeepers who did wail, "What, again!?" And they had a point.

And history continued its farcical cycle. But Dave saw it not. For only when all the Nikes in Footlocker have gone, and every poor bloody shopkeeper has lost the lot, and 50% of inner city youth has done time, will we realise that he just doesn't care about us.

We had a big day off when I was small,
Someone wrote 'stuff the wedding' on a car
park wall.
It was about a girl with big bloomers and a
see-through skirt,
And a bloke with big ears and a nicely
pressed shirt.
As she walked up the aisle in a crumpled dress,
We sat in the garden and had egg and cress.
They duly produced an heir and a spare,
Then she sat on her own and he lost his hair.
They both got around and the babies got bigger,
The spare turned out ginger and we tried not
to snigger.
It ended in phone taps, headlines and divorce,
So she went to the shops and he got on his horse.
Start the car, Henri, before we're missed,
As you wish, your highness, but I'm far too pissed.
Run rabbit run, the Di is cast,
As a reporter's car couldn't get past.
Crocodile red tops cry their princess is gone,
Dupes at the gates and Elton fucking John.
All they give is a circus and they take our bread,
And demand our obedience when they die or
get wed.
Here we go again wearing a familiar ring,
Now it's my turn to write 'stuff the wedding'.

rabelaisian

"So François, are you aware of why we have asked you here today?"

"I go to see a great perhaps?"

"Ooookaaay... perhaps we'd better simply get down to business. A complaint has reached us regarding your conduct about the office..."

"The wise may be instructed by a fool."

"Be that as it may, we have been made aware that some of your remarks have been inappropriate. This is not to mention your overly-physical interactions with your assistant."

"Gestures, in love, are incomparably more attractive, effective and valuable than words."

"Whatever... look François, we are going to have to let you go..."

"Bring down the curtain, the farce is played out."

"Just get out please François..."

racism

I am racist, but when I hear people speaking in a foreign language, I can't help wanting to know what they are saying. I know they aren't talking about me or anything, but sometimes it frustrates me that they might know a secret I will never understand. This should make me angry, my dad hates it when he hears people gibbering away, but I'm just curious. When I was 14 I got a book on Urdu from the library, had to hide it under my bed, but every night I read under my quilt by the light of a torch made in China. Some of the words were far too difficult, the syllables didn't make any sense and when I tried to whisper them to myself they made me spit. Dad says buying stuff from places like China is OK, because it *keeps the bastards working for us*. He's funny like that, says he hates anyone who isn't white, but thinks that we shouldn't be getting our hands dirty making things. He says we are the consumers, the top of the pile. Some of his mates say you should only buy British, but he says *we've been there and done that*, whatever that means. Anyway, when Dad found the book he made me burn it in the garden and we never went back to the library.

A few days later it was burnt down by some of the skins, I watched from my window and could feel the heat on my face.

regeneration (1)

The angle is all wrong. I am driving down the hill,
and the glare is still getting to me. I try to avoid his
eye, but I can't. The world revolves around him, his
face, his eye. Family eh, who'd have them? Christ!
You think a drive in the country would shake him
off, but no, no chance of that. No dignity for a god,
you'd think that would be important but he's old
now. Times are tough, and he isn't too proud for
a slow desperate crawl through the mud and dog
shit. Yes, he's there, skimming the surface of the
ground. The desperate nonchalance doesn't fool,
I'm not playing along. But neither is he, this is life
and death. But it's always like this at Yule time.
Bouncing through dead cold branches, the light
filters down, everywhere, reflecting off the runoff
from the blocked drains. The stream, the gold, my
father, who art in heaven. I ran from him in Egypt,
but how far can you run from a god?

The solstice today, longest night. He is a jealous
one, you know, gets worse at Christmas. I can feel
it start, my eyes, windows of the soul. A burning,
bright oxidation of the air. Yuletide greed, like
a pig at the trough. Stuff your face, digest, rust.
Atoms and molecules rush along, feet and arms
spread. John Barleycorn is no match for Osiris. The
burn, the scorch marks, the deafening finality of it
as I leave the road. I hope the engine doesn't go up
as well, or this will all be for nothing.

A 'cool fire', a controlled burn, won't scorch the
earth. It leaves room for others to grow. It really
should be done in the spring or the autumn. But
needs must and all that. And this is the shortest
night, the least sunlight. I have to make room for it.
New shoots need breathing space.

When a new transport hub is implanted into an old neighbourhood it is akin to a form of post-modernist invasive surgery. A PPP physician inserting gleaming titanium into wrecked degenerating tissue. While it will certainly ease movement it cannot heal the fractures of Zone 3. It only makes for an easier escape route. Only 15 minutes to Liverpool Street for man-bag porters and wheeled-luggage handlers. Step free access. Wipe-clean stainless steel and orange plastic emblazoned with the unmistakable imperial blue roundel and red cross stripe. An illuminated symbol that is the only admissible evidence of a more romantic past. Of any past. It has survived the dissolution of time that began in 1997 and hence it makes moths of us all. It makes the foolish heart ache for the sight of it through monochrome rain, the spots of which only increase its emotional pull.

Across the High Road, Buddleia forests flourish at right angles 30ft from the ground, interspersed with drying tea towels and the flags of various nations. The remains of exotic fish from the market lie in the gutter, paddled there on the soles of old ladies' fur-lined boots. Ranting street preachers wage their rap battles outside of cafés wafting the aroma of frying chicken.

Pavement princesses on unfeasible heels raise pencilled eyebrows higher than their hemlines at leery lads bobbing out of the precinct.

Shug frowns at three across and chugs his Guinness, anchored arm stuck out the window of The Railway as passers-by negotiate the tip of his Benson, which is technically breaking no law.

Above it all stares down the cold sprayed eyes of Monkey. Surveying this scene dispassionately as we apes pay no heed to this alien obelisk transplanted into our moonscape. Come the morning the courted achievers emerge fearful from their boltholes. To scurry through streets they may make no claim to lest they be claimed, pouring in tribute through its gates.

revolution

Half past three on a Sunday afternoon, she smiles at her grandson as he plays out back, as she makes sandwiches for school the next day. Think on this a while. Now compare it to a broken bottle, shattered on a car park floor. Have you noticed there are no similarities between these disparate images, but that the mind instantly jumps to fill gaps with no significant purpose or logical benefit? Maybe you haven't, but I suspect this will lead to a suspicion that either your brain works differently than most people's or that I am a liar. Both are possibilities, but of course, I may have been right all along.

My Medway driving instructor is much younger than he sounds on the phone, but he's got a confident air. He's clearly driven with frightened new drivers before, which puts me at ease. His mother is a friend of my mother-in-law, so I figure that he won't be able to declare me impossible right off the bat.

"Good stuff," my instructor says often during our hour and a half lessons. "Good stuff".

I think this is his very kind way of saying; "Thank you so much for not killing me today even though we went up over the sidewalk three times and you almost hit half the parked cars".

Either that or he can't think of anything I've done right, hence the general declaration of some positive elements existing somewhere.

Somewhere.

After two lessons my new mantra is: "The roundabout is your friend, the roundabout is your friend". I don't believe it for a second, and my cortisol levels shoot up to eleven every time I approach these innocuous-sounding circles of hell.

I get in the car with my instructor each week making every attempt to hide my certainty that I will meet my death squashed between motorists bound for Tesco and Rainham. I've driven long enough on the other side of the road to know, in my creaky bones, that this driving on the other side of the road thing is just wrong.

"We're all gonna die," I think, flying around what I hope is the right lane.

Good stuff, good stuff.

seedy (1)

He licks his lips like
A leopard who's been living
On lentils and leeks

seedy (2)

A large painting hangs in a dull lit room. It shows a naked woman running from a man, he is catching up, but as he reaches out her feet sprout roots and her fingers leaves, as she is transformed into a tree.

sophistication

When you pretend to like things that
you don't like, and/or understand things
you don't like, to people you don't know,
don't like, or understand either.

Seeking to justify
our togetherness.

We find meaning in the memory of
places we've both
been before we knew each other.
To validate our relationship's
part in the greater scheme
of things.

A gig in London, a street we
both visited
on the same day.
A tall man wearing a tattered blue mohair jumper
standing outside The Screen on the Green,
smoking.
Was that you?
A glance too long from a woman with
long hair, like she almost recognised you,
but then decided she didn't know you.
Not yet.

Did we brush
past each
other that day and say excuse me — can I just—
can I just —
And then the thought vanished away to somewhere,
erased by the smile in your eyes.

Still, always the feeling I've met you some place
before.
Maybe in a dream...

Up and down
Round and round
The streets of Chatham Town
We should have a tram, wham, bam thank you
Ma'am
Mr and Mrs Oogles and their out-of-date stock
Nobody flocks
There anymore.
Who needs San Francisco? Or a disco?
When you live in the streets of Chatham Town.
Red and Brown
Turn that frown
Upside down
Rose'n'Crown
The streets where I was born.

tourist (1)

He came back slight and muttering
incomprehensibly, an urge to hug, but meaning
gone, as if speaking from some lost dimension.
Tanned and shaggy haired nature boy with
wild eyes, grunting niceties and hinting at
attachment. Unsure of what or where he travels
next. Thoughts of my own failed explorations,
put off for better times that came and yet I
stayed, for safety or perhaps for love. And if
the changes wrote on him, would mark the
damage done — the journeys of the mind can
seem a greater destination. It is the mind that
scars the most, and eyes spoke closely of those
fractured synapses.

Internal trips can lose you too, so maybe best
to stop.

In Wales we noticed
There are more war memorials
Or maybe the war memorials are just
More obvious.
A relic to an earlier time.

Roads where there is an impossibility of walking
And the car is King,
Queen and Prime Minister too.
And it takes over an hour
To get to Chester on the bus.

In Wales we noticed
Everyone speaks with a Scouse accent
At least in Flintshire
Overlooking the River Dee and Birken'ead.

In Wales we noticed
Buildings closed, shutters outside
Rusting in the wet cold.
Boarded up and smashed up pubs and houses,
Every third one
Or so it seemed.

In Wales we noticed
Grand old red brick, pink and greige granite
Gothic buildings
With royal crests, municipal crests
Empty
Now first floor offices
To let.

In Wales we noticed
A white bridge like a harp.

town hall (1)

Basil Lusch had been working for the Directorate of Power[1] for 22 years, since the time of private provision, although this was never openly spoken of. It was interesting, he would often muse (to himself naturally), the extent to which the human mind could dissemble when necessary.

Gradually, over the past few years, he realised that it hardly ever crossed his mind. There had once been a furious battle of ideas over such things. Now there was no longer even a whispered conversation.

Citizens would sometimes, possibly out of a heady mix of desperation and substance-fuelled bravery, call and attempt to remind him of the past. He and his colleagues were furnished with a prepared script for such occasions that would admit no mention of such things. They would then pass on the number to the relevant Directorate.

Basil chuckled to himself as he logged out for the day. They'd had it all wrong, the protestors against the 'empower' acts. The threat of a police cell had become seen as vulgar and ineffective (although of course it still went on). Far better to take away someone's creature comforts from a safe distance. No-one saw that coming. He certainly hadn't. Just lucky to be working for the right team, eh?

Still, they can't see inside your head. At least, not yet anyway, he mused as he strode Friday-like past saluting security guards, through the retination gate. His actual views about such affairs remained a matter for himself and Gert alone. Some people rumoured that walls really did have ears. Basil knew it.

Still, sod all that. Best to assume that if his

thoughts were his own, his words were not, and shut the fuck up about it. The D13 would sweep him home to the heart of him for a weekend of mild abandon with Gertie. Well, it rhymes with dirty he thought. It must be the combination of boredom and vibration that inexorably make people's minds wander to sex on trams.

He was as close to skipping as a man of his years ever gets as he left the tram at The Parkway. It was the same every Friday. Through the arch of white Buddleia that Gert had planted all those years ago. The door buzzed and de-magnetised as he almost leapt over the threshold hollering: "Hi honey, I'm home!" in his kitsch American square accent he always used. It still made Gert smile. At least it would have if she were there.

Gert was currently unable to move a muscle. Deprived even of the power to move her own eyelids she had no option but to watch the scene being played out in front of her. Time seemed to slow as Basil's familiar goofy smile slid from his face. Second by second. Frame by frame. Then realisation. Then panic.

Her only possible response a single tear as Basil ran from their house. Fade to black.

[1] *What remained of organised Socialism as the C21 wore on eventually achieved a somewhat pyrrhic victory regarding the re-nationalisation of key industries. Successive failures by private finance to ensure basic service standards, particularly in times of war, led to the Emergency Powers Act of 2023. Provision of all utilities, transport, communications and food production was transferred to the military. This was not what they had been hoping for.*

town hall (2)

Grimy black and white façade, flickering in the grim daylight. The morally compromised hero stalks the tacky steps. The femme fatale catches his eye from inside, swishes her hair in disgust, sidles up to the plump mayor. Chump. He's not even sure why he came. Damn it! He's forgot his interior monologue. It begins to rain.

underbelly

Tickling his exposed flesh with a bloodied crow's feather. His stomach stretched out with handcuffs above his head, eyes bulging with pleading ecstasy.

Another satisfied customer.

underclass (1)

Deep below it squirms upon its slime coated
belly, spreading its weight, extending tendrils
and sensors up towards the earth. Above, urchins
with shattered ideas are poorly programmed,
exposing their inadequacies and shaved of hopes
and dreams. The remnants are devoured by this
sullen beast, trapped by our ancestors with wings
clipped and fire extinguished. This mighty wrym
of legend, banished in a bargain of safety for
existence.

Sometimes a spark leaks upwards, but the fire is
quickly doused.

underclass (2)

To make the cake, put a bunch of flowers on the
table. Flower is the basis of the dish. Some flour
will cover the base quite nicely. Flour, eggs, beaten
liberally. Put one in the oven. Leave it to bake.
Meantime, cover the rest with rouge. Make up.

   Split down the middle, cream first then jam.
Spreads easily, or so I'm told. She'll learn better.
Victoria Sponge can be knocked up anytime.

Our neighbours keep an old newspaper (2005? 2004?) on the ledge by their door. The paper's morphed through various stages of mildew, bleaching, and freezing, but hasn't moved an inch the whole time I've lived here.

"It was there in 2006," my husband says, "When I bought the house."

Mildew patterns the chipped white paint of the neighbour's brick like a fragile tapestry. One could easily begin to see things happening in the pattern. I remember the story of the woman on the 'bed rest cure' who loses it, starts to see small people, animals (and was it mythical creatures?) escaping from the wallpaper.

"The mind supplies greenery," I decide, while walking down the block towards Barnsole Road, skirting piles of trash and discarded chairs.

Welcome, ginger beer can bird. Sofa sopping with rain: you be a boxwood. Fox-visited rubbish: why not — a dogwood tree. How about you be in bloom.

The mean streets of Medway; what holds this place together, this glorious sprawling mess, vibrant, unpredictable? How could the grey metropolis of Strood, Rochester, Chatham be welded to the sublime climes of Cliffe and Rainham? How did the whole Frankenstein's monster of a place just not drop off the face of the Earth and fall into the sea long ago, what keeps this place afloat?

Life will find a way. The roads cut through everything; sunken, treacherous and constantly changing midstream. The Medway is alive, beneath all the grime and discarded wrappers. The dust from the Dockyard is finally settling, with only the faint stirrings of the commuter trains to lift a few recent layers. The sinkholes pepper the whole area, but like the lungs of a smoker they're slowly clogging up. Natural selection at work, just pave them over for some car parks. The creature must move on.

Slowly, surely, the tentacles of the metropolis creep out. Like all living things, its needs must go beyond survival and consumption. Why crawl toward Noah's Ark, when there's Leysdown-on-Sea? Why not cut through Grubb Street, walk Plucks Gutter to get Loose, skim Pett Bottom, to get from Stiff Street to Heart's Delight.

Where else is there to go?

violence

A field of purple flowers. They grow wild where her body lay.

wasteland

The moon was in the bright blue sky today
Looking down on us with her silvery face.
My goddess Selene
Wondering whether her Endymion sleeps
peacefully
Or if his dreams are as troubled as mine,
By memories, hopes and fears.
She turns to us and moves the tides,
Pushing them away, drawing them on,
Pushing me away, drawing me on, for
Some say we are stardust and to the stars we will
return,
But I say, no, we will go back to the sea
For the sea is from where we came.
We are all water.

What else would explain the desire
To dance in the summer rain,
What else would explain the desire
To lie down in the sea foam and let it cleanse us.
What else explains the need to build cities on the
Bank of the river?
We are all water. We are drawn to her.

At night I watch her through my window,
Think about the twelve
Who stood upon her face
And looked into the endless dark.
Saw their watery planet,
Thought 'is that all it is?'
When they came back,
How nothing they would ever do again,
Could ever do again, would ever
Exceed that moment,
Haunted men dreaming endlessly of stars.
And how the rest of their lives
They must have felt her drawing
Them on, to return, and have welcomed her as
a friend
When the light slips away.

Is there another Earth
In another galaxy
Where another 'I' stands
Looking at the moon
In the daytime sky
And asks 'is there life on other planets?'

On another Earth
In another time
Did she point to the marvel in the sky
Show the townsfolk the sun and the moon
Then drowned for this unnatural urge, this
curiosity,
Return too soon to the water.

xenophobia (1)

She is unsure about him. He possesses an odour that although not unpleasant, distracts her from her world. If he just went away, it would make things much easier, but she needs him to fix the sink.

xenophobia (2)

For you there is only this moment, this thing that
you do right now,
This breath, this opinion you exhale so carelessly,
I see you on the train playing with your
newspaper, *'tells it like it is mate'*,
This editorial, weaving its lies so carefully,
If I could make this fire you play with real, I would
do it,
And by those burns you shall be seen.

You talk of our history, our race, the way things
were 20 years past,
But it is yours and yours alone, my little Englander.
It is a drop of rain, it came, it went, no more than
that,
If I could turn your words to shit so that you would
choke on them,
And feel its taste, I would do it, the stink never
fading,
And by its taint you shall be known.

You appeal to my accident of birth, accuse me of
treason,
Clearly mistaking me for one who is white as white
as you,
You seek a mirror, for all your prejudices, your
insecurities,
But that is not me, my confidante, for a colour is all
we share,
If I could make your thoughts tattoos I would do it,
This table turned,
And by your skin shall you be shunned.

youth (1)

I hung out with them for a while.
They talked to me for a summer or two.
But then it changed.

  I had thought they were my friends, but they
didn't call, they didn't visit, and then I moved
away, and didn't call them either.

  And as I look back from many years, I realise
now how I miss them.

youth (2)

Stasis. Caught between post-foetal helplessness and realisation of mature slavery. A time to express frustration at being neither a thing or no-thing. Potentiality.

In the footsteps of famous women we begin
to look at places anew. Interrogating the
statuary. Looking at place names. Seeking
out these sisters where they have been
immortalised in concrete and stone.

In Gravesend we look for traces of an Indian
princess; we find a mural opposite the train
station, we find a statue in the churchyard,
surrounded by laughing teenagers and
snapping tourists. Memorial window's dusty
sparkle in the fading mid-noon sun. A women
who only visited a place to die an early death,
but who now will live here forever in signage
and distorted cartoon memory.

In Dublin's fair city we can't find one famous
woman amongst the men who coldly keep
watch; pigeon-encrusted brass, marble and
stone faces looking on. Then, when we find her
in Grafton Street, what we see is just the
x-rated version of a fictional ditty, all 38DDs
and wheelbarra, no closer to finding any truth.

In deciding to pass the plans, approve the
drawings, cast the bronze, carve the marble;
making lasting things for us to gawp at, does
the objectifier briefly become the objectified?

Water is alluring; unstoppable, host
to strange and unfathomable
creatures. They sweep forward
on the tide, with liquid grace and
surface glitter. It dazzles; perfect
cover. Between them lurks the shark
buoyed up on
rivers of lager; a stranger lost in the depths,
vague glimmers of life dimly reflected in
shades of blue, green, the
latest shades;
a sharp relief of black and brown
shimmering in the depths
of yellow street lights.

Immersed, they split, join,
split; finally settling at the lowest
level of the street.
I freeze, a grey statue caught out of
time; overwhelmed. Scalding rivulets
join the irresistible current. I am not
crying: this is
nature, taking its course.
The strong eat the weak,
salt water corrodes, one
piece at a time.

appendix: the rules

i. No article should attempt to define its subject using any physical or descriptive characteristics or attributes. No thingness!

ii. Articles should celebrate the duality of THINGS and avoid the assumption that they have one fixed meaning.

iii. There must be beauty in the profane and filth in the sacred.

iv. Never mention the title of the article within the article.

v. Always criticise the task.

vi. Each article should be written in under 29 minutes and 36 seconds and may not exceed 593 words.

vii. If you are unclear about the rules then read the rules.

viii. **Destroy all structures and disobey the rules**.

Barry Fentiman is a Medway-based poet and mythogeographer who performs around the South East. His writing has been published in *The Medway Broadside*, *The Irish Post*, *Stories from songs* and *The Seed Catalogue*.

  ...*alienation (2), bourgeois, capital, clone-town, city without a head, concrete jungle, crime, derelict, desolation, energy (2), extremism (2), gentrification, generic, glow, haven, high rise, isolation(1), jersey-strip, keep, kudos, lost, metropolitan, neon, panopticon, paranoia, pavement, pollution, prostitution, protest (2), queen, rabelasian, regeneration (2), town hall (1), xenophobia (2).*

Sam Hall founded ME4Writers in 2009. She is a playwright whose plays have been performed internationally, and her writing has been published in *The Irish Post*, *The Lock*, *Theatre and Performance*, *WOWKent*, *Stories from songs*, and online magazines including *Remotegoat* and *SilverLion*. She also runs 17Percent, an organisation to promote equality in theatre writing.

  ...*architecture, business, busyness, cathedral, cctv, civic, commerce, commute, down town, fear, finance (2), friendship, graffiti, hive (1), identity, invisible, kaleidoscope, orbital (1), pigeon, protest (1), stranger, tourist (2), wasteland, youth (1), zoo.*

SM Jenkin Former chair of the Medway Mermaids, SM Jenkin has had work published in several anthologies including *The Mermaid*, *Medway Festival Fringe*, the *Medway Messenger*, and in publications including *Touchstone* and *Blithe Spirit*. SM's short